Coming Home

Written by Tu Vuong

Illustrated by Alejandro Contreras

Coming Họmẹ
Written by Tu Vuong
Illustrated by Alejandro Contreras
Published by EduMatch®
PO Box 150324, Alexandria, VA 22315

www.edumatch.org

sarah@edumatch.org

ISBN: 978-1-953852-83-0

My heart and my home

———————————————

———————————————

| Preface

Deconstructing memory can be a delicate process. It can serve to connect, disconnect and heal all at once. The events here are written in short, poetic verses to capture moments in time. They have been my own experiences along with my family; many of the details have been pieced together from childhood memories, personal stories that have been passed from one generation to the next as well as conversations with family members. Each event chronicled in this book is uniquely significant in that each person experiences, interprets and recalls it in a way that makes sense to them in their ever-changing contexts. That is our being.

These vignettes are intended to echo a piece of the immigrant experience as well as to affirm the importance of our identity. This book can be read in sequence or each poem can be a pause for reflection. The style is congruous, with a subtle play on words to convey meaning that is both literal and abstract — a story to be enjoyed through its imagery and an intimate connection to each moment.

| Part I | Heart

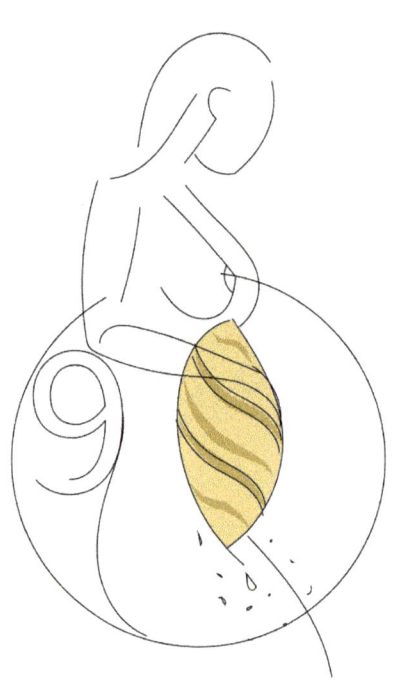

A day and nine months
with only a bite of *bánh* in her belly
she breathed in
pushed
so that I may breathe out
into the world.

| Bread of life

Fragments
of *Tết* lanterns burned
the children gamboled
they sang
they cried
they stumbled
upon limp bodies
in the playground
from the debris
of the bombings
mistakenly
intended for the enemy -

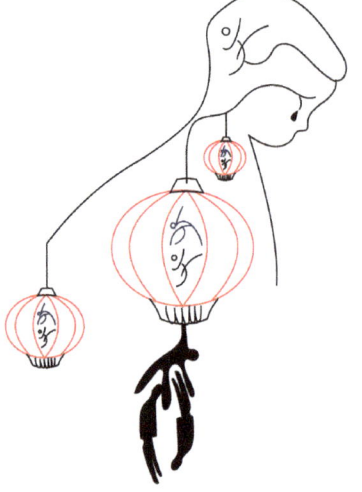

The drum at dusk,
their hearts stopping
momentarily
only to examine
if the faces were familiar.

| Tears of solace among corpses

My mother's family hastened
from the north to the south

My father's family secured plans
to send my grandmother to safety

They became neighbours
in the heart of *Saigon*

My mother, a teacher
my father, a geologist

She couldn't teach him
how to love

He couldn't carve out
a heart from stone

With the war looming
and the warning bells ringing

They learned to support each other
from the ground up

They learned to survive -
was it love?

| Somewhere in between your head and your heart

There won't be milk for several days -
Two and taken aback,
I pleaded persistently
threatening harm
to myself
all a ruse
but
intrinsically revealing
how much
I ingested
the noise that
surrounded me.

Unbeknownst
to me
was that in
fourteen days
my mother
was planning to escape
our country
by foot
on a secretly
marked trail
towards Cambodia
in the dead of night.

Việt Nam
a once resource-rich place
my parents called home.

| Gut-wrenching resilience

Come here -
no!
Khmer!
Don't go near
it's a nightmare
my dear
fear
reared.

Rouge.

Genocide.

| My father's dream, what saved us that night

Pirates
in the South China Sea
might have robbed
the innocent
seeking refuge
of their life's savings
but not their worth -
their dignity
and
indignation
provided strength
to survive the harrowing
sea passage
in the end
to see themselves
utmost dignified.

| We survived a war, we will survive this too

Eighty-four -
crammed into a wooden craft
were attacked three times,
some abducted
during the eight days at sea.

Dehydrated and desperate
the remaining survivors
clung tightly
to each other,
for each other.

A glimmer of hope
glistened the waters
as they were rescued
by workers
from a German freighter.

That night
from a distance
they stood and watched
as their vessel sank
into the sea.

But their collective spirit was lifted.

| They would later be called the *boat people*

The regime boasted
re-education,
re-habilitation,
re-integration -

The only true reform
was re-formed
when the people came together
reunited and re-built.

| *Saigon* rises

My mother packed our lives into a suitcase.

| Two days until we would reunite with my father and brother in Canada

Goodbye,
one day I'll be coming home
to you
but
will you embrace me?

| Leaving my heart in a country whose spirit I will finally admire one day

| Part II | Spirit

Saint Patrick,
the beginning
of my immigration story -

Courage.

Marion Dewar,
the beginning
of my journey story -

Purpose.

My mother,
the beginning
of my life story -

Strength.

| Gratitude juxtaposed

For months
around our kitchen table
O Canada
was a discord
of accented karaoke
rattling along a half-broken
cassette recorder
with each person
reciting for our
citizenship
misplacing the stress
in each word
changing its meaning
to an anthem
we never understood
in the first place.

| Singing out of tune with our new life

You tried
until you were tired
and every night
I would lie awake
until I heard
the front door open
and the familiar tempo
of your footsteps
treading softly
up the stairs
to sleep.

I tried
until I was tired
to be perfect
but inside I was not,
abandonment misunderstood
I knew you were weary
working relentlessly
on the line
for us all
to have a warm bed
to sleep.

We tried
until we were tired.

Gia đình.

| Living in harmony with family

On Fridays
we slowed down -
crossing the street
holding your hand
looking up to you
singing a rhyme from school
walking to the supermarket
getting the week's staples
treating me to a slice of pizza
indulging in a caramel candy.

I was beaming.

Every Friday
was my day
with you.

| Joy

You should be grateful
You should feel safe
You should learn
our language.

Our?
Do you mean yours?
Perhaps it is you
and not I.

You should assimilate
Do you mean annihilate?

You should
I could
but
what if I told you otherwise?

| Unpromised land

Họ...family name
Mẹ...mother

Three generations in one household -

Otherwise known as home.

| What do other families look like?

You adored me
even more
when I ran out the door
leaving you torn
but you endured
the hurt
sure
that one day
your sore
would be my soar!

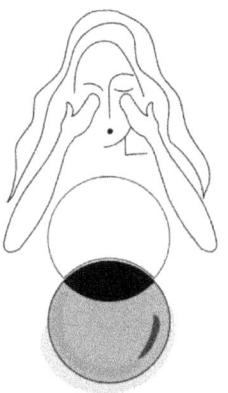

| A teenager caught in two cultural worlds

Two drinks
to decelerate
from the week -

Four.

Six.

Eight.

Accelerate.

The mood became somber
and we often wondered
what would happen if you had two more?

On the brink.

| Cycle of everything you hate

Tú.

My name.

My identity.

My heritage.

It doesn't matter
to you
how you say it
as long as I say
I am grateful.

You glorify me
when it's convenient.

It doesn't matter
to you
how I say it
as long as I say
I am grateful.

Ask me
how to say it.

My name.

My identity.

My heritage.

But not where I am from -

Gratefulness is mine to give
not yours to expect.

Just like your acceptance.

| Underlying conditions

Seoul was my sign.

Becoming.

| A journey of soul-searching

| Part III | Soul

Holding my history
and
telling my story
from the present
moment
no longer gasping
tangled in my past
or grasping for my future
but
ever evolving.

Resonance.

| In sync with myself

Being away
has a way
of opening
your heart to feel
what had always been
in front of your eyes -

I just couldn't see it.

I couldn't see him.

Behind the wall
was anger, violence -
heartache
heartbreak.

Until he was broken.

| PTSD, effects of war

You only lose what you cling to
a borrowed adage
but the most profound lesson
I've held on to.

Changes.

| Letting go

Clarity has come from
taking a step back
to appreciate the details.

Looking inward.

| Insight

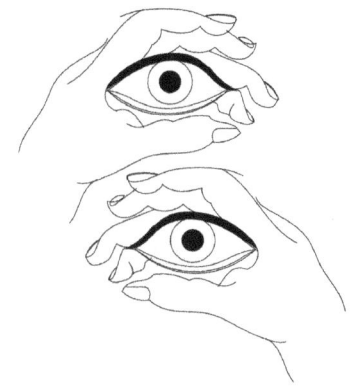

Without sounding
like a cliché
they say
there's always
a teacher
who leaves an imprint.

If it weren't for you
I would still be high
but not on life.

| Connectedness, why I am a teacher today

Dear students,

Let's break the barriers
beyond these bare
white walls
and teach me
the magnitude of your greatness.

| Your story is the soul in each lesson

Two hearts
one spirit
You can make it anywhere.

Hear her voice,
I'm leaving today -
singing
every February
as she continues to resound
and live
through the beat
of your footsteps
every day.

| Friendships that dance within me

My parents call me once a week -
What have you eaten today?

My mother messages me photos of a traditional dish -
What have you eaten today?

My father texts me a new vintage Cabernet -
What have you eaten today?

I am 42.

| Food is a language of love

Time itself doesn't heal.

Giving a voice to my emotions
was the hardest conversation
I had to have with myself.

| Inner critic

What's been
is behind me -

Not apart from me
but a part of me.

What stands
before me
is bestowed
on me
so that I may
become
and
breathe in
the beauty
of my entire being.

| Be

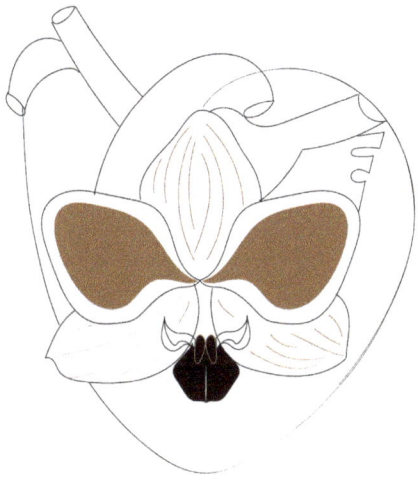

About the Author

Tu Vuong is an educator who has worked in a number of capacities including consultant, teacher and advocate for newcomer families and students. She has been a lead in projects with the Ontario Ministry of Education, Apple Education, and has contributed numerous educational content to various magazines, blogs and podcasts. She currently resides in Ottawa, Canada.

www.ingramcontent.com/pod-product-compliance
Lightning Source LLC
Chambersburg PA
CBHW051650120626
46551CB00015B/2301